A Story of the Chinese Zodiac

This is MY Year!

The Fire Horse

2026

A Keepsake Book of Self-Discovery

First Edition

Mentor NYC

This book is a work of fiction and cultural storytelling. While inspired by mythology, folklore, and historical traditions, all characters, events, and interpretations are presented for educational and inspirational purposes. Any resemblance to actual persons, living or dead, is purely coincidental.
The Chinese zodiac and related cultural traditions are shared here with respect and curiosity. Interpretations of zodiac traits are meant for reflection and encouragement only and should not be taken as scientific, medical, or predictive advice. Every child is unique.

First edition.
ISBN: 979-8-9985337-7-8
LCCN: 2026902011
Printed in United States

Published by:
Mentor NYC LLC
New York, NY
United States
www.mentornyc.org

"The moment you doubt whether you can fly,
you cease forever to be able to do it."

— J. M. Barrie
from Peter Pan

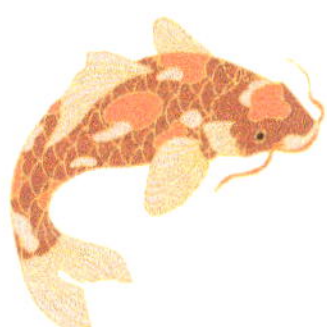

Throughout the book, traditional Chinese symbols of luck, fortune, and prosperity are hidden.
Find as many as you can and keep all the blessings!

This book is a gift for someone very special—worthy of a star in the Hall of Fabulousness—named...

(drumroll, please)

CONTENTS:

Prologue 1

Introduction 5

The Chinese Zodiac: A Magical Calendar of Animals 7
- The Question: *Is It Science? Is It Myth?* 9
- Did You Know? 12

The Five Elements: More Than Animals 13
- The Big Idea: *A Symbol or A Label?* 17
- A Gentle Reminder: *Shining Outside or Sleeping Inside* 18
- Quick Test: *What Element of Horse Are You?* 19

The Ancient Story: Jade Emperor's Summon 23

Enchanting Horses: How They Ruled The Mythical World 31
- Quick Test: *Which Mythical Horse Are You?* 82

Legendary Horses: In History and In Real Life 87

A Hoof-Powered City: Horses in New York's History 91
- Horses and Central Park 94
- Did You Know? 96
- Scavenger Hunt: *When You Visit Central Park* 98
- Quick Quiz: *Horses in Central Park* 99

Hooves to Engines: The Horsepower Continues 101
- How Horses Became Engines 103
- Quick Quiz: *Which Horse-Inspired Car Are You?* 109

Polo: The Sport of Kings 113
- Did You Know? 117

Fun & Quirky Horse Facts 119

Want More?: Horse Museums & Exhibits 121

The Message: For the "Horse Year" Children 123
- Quick Quiz: *What Horse Trait Do You Have?* 125

Scavenger Hunt: Symbols of Luck & Fortune 129

Coming Up Next 133

The Publisher 134

PROLOGUE

Welcome to This Is MY Year — Year of the Fire Horse, a celebration of motion, courage, and unstoppable energy. This book begins with an ancient system that has guided lives for thousands of years: the Chinese zodiac—a twelve-year cycle where each year is shaped by an animal's spirit and refined by one of five elements.

Among them, the Horse stands apart as the symbol of freedom, speed, independence, and bold forward movement. When paired with Fire, that spirit ignites into something extraordinary: passion, confidence, creativity, and a refusal to stand still.

But this is not just a book about astrology.
It is a story about why horses have always mattered to humans—and why they still do today.
Created for children born in the Year of the Horse in the lunar calendar, this book also invites young readers to discover their own strengths, trust their inner energy, and realize their full potential.

Across cultures and centuries, horses have leapt from history into legend. From heavenly steeds that crossed the skies, to loyal warhorses that changed the fate of empires, to enchanted horses that tested heroes and carried dreams, these animals became mirrors of our greatest hopes and fears.

Here, you'll encounter mythical and enchanting horses from around the world, discovering how different civilizations used horse legends to explain bravery, loyalty, ambition, and the cost of power.

As the world modernized, hooves became wheels. Muscles became engines. The very idea of horsepower was born from our attempt to measure motion against the strength of a living horse. Some of today's most iconic automobiles—names like Mustang, Bronco, and Prancing Horse—carry that legacy forward, proving that even in steel and speed, we still chase the spirit of the horse.

This journey also brings us to New York, a city once powered almost entirely by horses. Before subways and taxis, horses shaped the streets, parks, bridges, and daily life—and even thrilling sports like polo, the "King's Game," were played in and around the city.

From Central Park's carriage drives to long-vanished stables and lasting traditions, NYC's bond with horses is woven into its story, reminding us that every fast-moving future starts with a strong past.

If you were born in the Year of the Horse, you'll explore what makes you who you are—your strengths, challenges, instincts, and inner fire. Whether you are a natural leader, a restless explorer, a creative force, or a quiet runner with a powerful stride, the Horse offers a language for understanding yourself and your momentum in the world.

This is a book about movement. About knowing when to run free—and when to hold the reins.

This isn't just a year on the calendar.

This is your year.

恭喜發財

Introduction:
Once upon a very busy year...

In 2014, the ***Year of The Wood Horse***, babies were popping into the world everywhere—so many that if you lined them all up, they'd circle the Earth more than once!

Around 140 million babies were born across the globe that year. In the United States alone, nearly 4 million little stars arrived—each one with their own special spark.

Now here's where the magic begins...

If you were born on or between ***January 31, 2014 and February 18, 2015***, the ancient Chinese zodiac says you were born under the sign of the (wait for it...) WOOD HORSE.

Wood Horses are known for being curious, energetic, kind-hearted, and full of big ideas—always ready to explore the world and help others along the way like a strong leader.

And galloping toward the future...

Children born on or between February 17, 2026, and February 5, 2027, will be known as FIRE HORSES—bold, daring, and filled with passion! Fire Horses radiate brilliance, embrace adventure, and possess hearts ablaze with courage and confidence.

According to historical trends, over 130 million babies may be welcomed into the world during this time.

Wherever they come into this world, these Fire Horse children bring a luminous sense of hope—reminding us that each new year offers fresh energy, boundless possibilities, and a new generation to sprint toward the future.

The Chinese Zodiac:
A Magical Calendar of Animals

Long ago, people in China began to notice something curious about time. It didn't just move forward—it returned, again and again.

Patterns appeared. Stories repeated.

To capture this hidden rhythm, they created something magical: the Chinese Zodiac—a living calendar made of twelve animals, each with its own personality, strengths, and stories to tell.

In this calendar, years aren't counted by numbers alone. Instead, each year is guarded by an animal. One follows the next in a fixed order, and when the twelfth animal finishes its turn, the cycle begins all over again—forming a never-ending circle of time, where every year carries a familiar spirit, yet welcomes brand-new beginnings.

Today, scientists explain time using astronomy, math, and calendars that track the movement of the Earth, Moon, and Sun.

The Chinese Zodiac isn't necessarily a scientific rule—it's a belief system and storytelling tradition that people have shared for thousands of years to help make sense of time, personality, and change.

The 12 Zodiac Animals (in order) are:
Rat • Ox • Tiger • Rabbit • Dragon • Snake • Horse • Goat • Monkey • Rooster • Dog • Pig

Each animal represents certain traits—ideas people have passed down for centuries about how we may think, act, and respond to challenges.

The Question:
Is It Science? Is It Myth?

People also noticed something else interesting: kids born in the same year often seemed to share similarities.

In ancient China, scholars took this idea seriously. They carefully studied the sun, moon, stars, and planets, along with calendars and seasons. They believed that when you were born—your year, season, and even the time of day—placed you inside a giant cosmic pattern, like a rhythm the whole universe followed.

This wasn't just guessing or magic. Many people (especially in Asia) respected it as a real field of study that mixed astronomy, math, nature, and philosophy, although not everyone agreed.

Some people think kids born in the same year are similar simply because they:

- Grow up experiencing same major changes and events in the world
- Use the same tools or technology and are affected by the same factors such as culture, habit, etc. since young age

In other words, it might *not* be the stars—it could be just shared experiences and environment.

However, a question remained:
Where do our personalities really come from? How much of who we are is shaped by nature—and how much by how we are raised?

That's why many people still believed that time itself told a story. The exact year, season—even the hour you were born—was thought to place you inside a vast pattern shared by the entire universe. You weren't random. *You were part of a design.*

To understand this design, scholars became careful observers. They watched the sun and moon, tracked the stars, counted days on calendars, and studied how seasons changed.

This wasn't just guessing or superstition—it shaped real life, including:

- When farmers planted and harvested crops
- How people thought about health and medicine
- When to hold weddings, choose names for babies, or make important decisions

Over time, thinkers created systems like the *I Ching* and the *Four Pillars of Destiny*.

These weren't spells or magic tricks. They used math, symbols, and careful observation to explain personality, balance, and timing in life. People studied and passed down these ideas for hundreds of years.

For some, the charts and calculations were hard to understand. So people came up with a clever shortcut. They used animals. Each animal stood for a trait—brave, patient, clever, steady. Instead of boring charts or hard math, they used a tiger, a dragon, or a horse to make big ideas easy to remember.

And there were experts who studied these patterns. They weren't just mysterious people at market stalls. They advised kings and queens, helped families pick important dates, and traveled along trade routes like the Silk Road.

Did You Know?

- Ancient Chinese calendars were so accurate that farmers used them to decide when to plant crops.
- The zodiac system is over 2,000 years old—older than most countries today!
- In traditional Chinese thought, time moves in cycles, not straight lines, which is why zodiac animals repeat.

- Some people still look at zodiac dates today, especially when they feel nervous about the future. They hope it might give them a small peek at what's ahead. It isn't an exact science, but it can work like a guide or a hint—something to think about, not something that decides everything.
- Chinese astrology and related services are a huge business in the global market worth many billions.

The Five Elements: *More Than Animals*

Thousands of years ago, people didn't count time with watches or printed calendars. They watched the sky.

Ancient Chinese astronomers carefully observed:

- The Sun (for seasons)
- The Moon (for months)
- The planets, especially one slow-moving bright star that stood out from the rest

That "star" was actually Jupiter.
Jupiter takes about 12 years to travel once around the sky. To ancient observers, this made it the perfect cosmic clock.

So instead of asking, "What year is it?" people asked:
"Which year of Jupiter's journey are we in?"
That was the beginning of the 12-year cycle.

Just like there are the Sun, the Moon, and the Stars in the sky, there are Five Elements in the world:
Wood, Fire, Water, Earth, and Metal

Trees grew, burned, returned to soil.
Rivers shaped land.
Metal formed from stone.
Nothing stayed the same—but nothing disappeared either.

These weren't just materials you could touch—they were energies, always moving and transforming.

Wood was born first. It stood for growth, beginnings, and creativity—like seeds pushing through the ground.

Fire followed, bright and powerful. It represented energy, courage, and change—the spark that turns ideas into action.

Earth came next, calm and steady. Earth meant balance, patience, and support—the place where everything could rest and grow strong.

Metal emerged from the Earth, strong and sharp. It stood for focus, discipline, and determination—the power to shape and protect.

Water flowed last, quiet but unstoppable. Water symbolized wisdom, adaptability, and reflection—moving around obstacles instead of breaking.

The elements didn't compete. They worked together, flowing in a circle:
Wood feeds Fire.
Fire creates Earth (ash).
Earth forms Metal.
Metal enriches Water.
Water nourishes Wood.

And so the Five Elements became a way to understand time, nature, and people—a reminder that life is always changing, but always connected.

Ancient observers used their observations of the repeating patterns as a symbolic language to explain change in the world and in people.

Wood – growth, kindness, creativity

Fire – passion, bravery, confidence

Earth – stability, honesty, patience

Metal – strength, focus, determination

Water – wisdom, imagination, flexibility

And something extra special happens when an animal and an element come together—like *Wood Horse* or *Fire Dragon*—they create a special combination that only happens every 60 years! (Think of all the combinations when 12 animals meet 5 elements!)

Combine that with details like the month, the day, and even the hour of birth—and suddenly, how many possible combinations are there? People believed each detail added another layer, like mixing many colors to create a brand-new shade. That's why two children born in the same animal year could still grow into very different people.

And beyond the calendar, there were other forces too—the family they were born into, the place they grew up, the challenges they faced, and the choices they made. While a birthday (and even a birth time) might explain part of who someone is, every person becomes their own unique self, with a story no chart can fully capture.

The Big Idea:
A Symbol or A Label?

Each zodiac animal is just a symbol, not a label. The traits linked to each sign are meant to remind people of hidden potentials—strengths that might already be shining brightly... or quietly waiting inside.

The zodiac whispers:
"Remember, the power is already inside you. Believe in it—and let it shine."

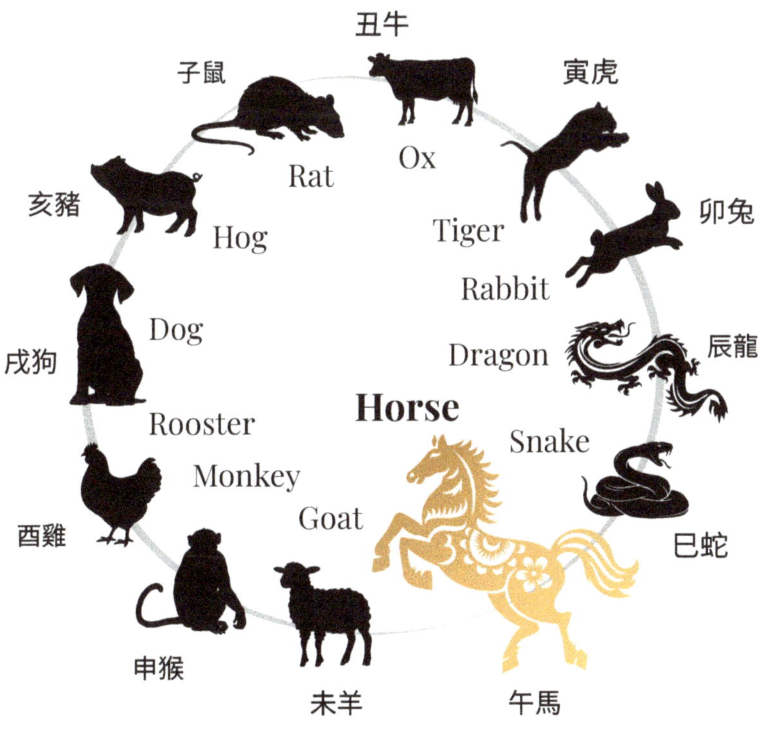

A Gentle Reminder: *Shining Outside or Sleeping Inside*

Not everyone shows their strengths in the same way.

- A brave person may speak up loudly—or stay calm in hard moments.
- A creative person may draw—or solve problems in clever ways.
- A leader may stand in front—or help others shine.

Remember, you are your own person.
Two people born in the same year can be completely different.

Why? Because who you become is shaped by:

- Your choices
- Your family and friends
- Your experiences
- Your hard work

The zodiac is meant to spark curiosity and imagination, not to decide who you are or what you are meant to become. Enjoy it, explore it, learn from it—but don't take it as a limit.

The most important part of your story is still the *choices* you make.

Quick Test:
What Element of Horse Are You?

Answer each question by choosing the option that feels most like you!

Keep track of the letter you pick most often.

1. When you start something new, you prefer to...

A. Learn slowly and improve as you go
B. Jump in with excitement
C. Make sure everyone feels comfortable
D. Set a clear goal and stick to it
E. Watch first, then adjust

2. Your biggest strength is...

A. Growing and helping others grow
B. Energy and confidence
C. Reliability and patience
D. Determination and focus
E. Understanding people and situations

3. When problems appear, you usually...

A. See them as chances to learn
B. Face them head-on
C. Stay calm and steady
D. Push through until they're solved
E. Find another path around them

4. Which place feels most like you?

A. A forest or garden
B. A bright sunrise or campfire
C. Open land or a mountain
D. A strong bridge or fortress
E. A river, lake, or ocean

5. In a group, you often...

A. Encourage new ideas
B. Motivate others
C. Keep things balanced
D. Take responsibility
E. Listen carefully

6. When something doesn't go your way, you...

A. Try again with a new approach
B. Keep going with passion
C. Stay patient
D. Push yourself harder
E. Adapt and change direction

7. What matters most to you?

A. Growth
B. Passion
C. Stability
D. Strength
E. Flow

8. People trust you because you are...

A. Supportive
B. Inspiring
C. Dependable
D. Strong-willed
E. Flexible

Your Horse Element

Mostly A — Wood Horse
You grow with time. You love learning, creativity, and helping ideas—and people—become stronger.

Mostly B — Fire Horse
You shine brightly. You are bold, passionate, and full of energy. When you believe in something, others feel it too.

Mostly C — Earth Horse
You are steady and grounding. People rely on you for balance, patience, and calm strength.

Mostly D — Metal Horse
You are focused and determined. You value discipline, strength, and finishing what you start.

Mostly E — Water Horse
You are adaptable and thoughtful. You understand change and move wisely through it.

2008
2020
2009
2021
2010
2022
2011
2023
2012
2024
2013
2025
2014
2026
2015
2027
2016
2028
2017
2029
2018
2030
2019
2031
MEOW!
HOW ABOUT ME!?

The Ancient Story: *Jade Emperor's Summon*

Before calendars.
Before clocks.
Before time had a name—
the heavens already had a ruler.
His name was the Jade Emperor.

From his celestial throne in a palace carved of clouds and starlight, the Jade Emperor looked down upon the restless world.

Seasons turned, and history flowed without markers.
Farmers argued over when to plant or harvest.
Travelers arrived too early—or far too late.
Festivals were celebrated twice... or missed entirely.
Children grew taller, elders grew wiser, yet no one could agree when it had happened.

Days slipped into nights. Years blurred together.
Time moved forward—but no one knew how to name it.

"I will give time a name and a story," he declared.
"The name will be earned by those who are brave enough to participate."

His voice echoed everywhere—
through forests, rivers, rooftops, and burrows—
reaching every creature who would soon learn
that time is shaped by action, not chance.

There would be the Great Race.

The first twelve animals to reach the celestial gate would rule the rhythm of years forever.

Every animal heard the call.
And every animal believed something different about how to answer it.

The Cat lifted her head from licking her elegant paw.
She disliked crowds, chaos, and rushing hearts.
All around her, animals packed and chatted and speculated—running in circles, bumping tails, panicking loudly.

The Rat is so alert, she thought.
And I'm sure he's very proud that I think of him as a friend.

With a graceful flick of her tail, the Cat tossed her half-eaten fish to the Rat and said,
"Wake me when it is time, my friend."

Then she curled herself beneath the moonlight, perfectly confident.
"You bet," said the Rat, smiling—already sniffing the fish.

Elsewhere, the choices were louder.
The Tiger sharpened his claws. *Strength will carry me.*

The Dragon rose into the clouds, scales glinting with pride. *Honor matters more than speed.*

And the Horse pawed the earth, muscles coiled, breath steady. *I will run*, he vowed, *until my spirit burns.*

The Ox lowered his head, calm and steady. *I will endure.*

And the Rat thought, quietly, *I am small. I have to outsmart everyone to beat these big, strong, and fast guys.*

The Cat curled her tail around her paws and stretched lazily.
I've got plenty of time for a nice, long nap, she murmured, smiling. *My good friend Rat will wake me when it's time.*

At dawn, the river roared to life.

The Ox stepped into the water without fear, pushing forward with patience and power.

He was strong, steady, and determined to cross on his own.

Just then, the Rat scampered up beside him. “Ox,” the Rat said quickly, bowing low, “your strength is unmatched. But my eyes are sharp, and my ears are keen. I can help you watch the current and warn you of danger.”

“If you can help,” the Ox said, “then climb on.” Before the Ox could change his mind, the Rat leapt onto his back, gripping tightly and staying perfectly still.

The Ox pushed through the river with steady strength, each step slow but unstoppable. The water splashed high against his sides, yet he never faltered.

All the while, the Rat clung tightly to the Ox’s back, hidden from view, counting every step. When the Ox’s hooves finally touched dry land, the Rat sprang into action. With a quick hop and a flash of his tail, he leapt down and darted ahead, landing at the gate a heartbeat before the Ox.

The Jade Emperor raised his hand, and the order was set—Rat first, Ox second. The Ox only blinked in surprise, then nodded calmly, accepting his place without complaint.

The Tiger plunged into the river next, muscles straining as he fought the powerful current. With a final roar, he reached the far bank and claimed third place.

Not far behind, the Rabbit bounded lightly from stone to stone, hopping across floating logs with quick feet and clever balance. Splashing only once, she landed safely on the other side, earning fourth place.

All eyes then turned to the sky. *Surely the Dragon would arrive first.* But instead, he appeared later, gliding gently down and taking only fifth place.

The Jade Emperor raised an eyebrow.
"Hmm... I thought you would arrive first," he said.
The Dragon bowed his head respectfully.
"On my way, I saw a village suffering from drought," he said. "I stopped to bring them rain. I also helped a friend cross the river."

The Jade Emperor's stern expression softened into a smile.
"Kindness matters," he said.
"You will not lead the years, but you will watch over the skies. When the world is dry, you will bring rain. When crops are in danger, you will protect them."

The Dragon bowed deeply.

The Horse charged into the river, hooves pounding, certain his speed would carry him ahead.
All the while, the Snake was already there—wrapped tightly around the Horse's leg, hidden beneath muscle and mane, letting the Horse do the work.

The Horse burst onto dry land and sprinted for the gate, sure he was alone.
Then—hiss!
In a flash, the Snake uncoiled and dropped in front of him. Startled, the Horse reared back for just a heartbeat.

That was enough.
The Snake slid across the line to claim sixth place, and the Horse followed a step behind in seventh.

The Goat, arrived eighth, quietly and graciously.

The Monkey, quick and clever, followed in ninth, and the Rooster, flapping and crowing proudly, came in tenth.

The loyal Dog paddled across at last, finishing eleventh.

Finally, with a happy grin and a very full belly, the Pig waddled to the finish line. He had stopped for snacks along the way, but he arrived just in time to claim the twelfth and final place.

The twelve places were filled.

Far away, beneath a warm patch of sunlight, the Cat suddenly opened her eyes.

"What?!" she cried. "Where is everybody?!"
She leapt to her feet and ran as fast as she could—but when she reached the river, it was already too late.

When the Cat learned that the Rat had never come to wake her, her heart sank. From that day on, she never forgave him. And that is why, even now, cats chase rats, and rats hide in the dark.

The Jade Emperor studied the twelve animals, and announced.
"You did not arrive by chance. You arrived by the choices you made."

Some moved with strength.
Some with patience.
Some with kindness.
Some with cleverness.
One relied too much on others to carry the way.

You don't choose where you begin, and you don't fully control where you end.
But you always choose *how* you move forward.
What matters most is *what* you believe
and *who* you choose to become.

Enchanting Horses:
How They Ruled The Mythical World

In the Great Race, the Horse mattered not because of tricks or shortcuts, but because of motion itself. While others paused to calculate or hide, the Horse ran—driven by heart, freedom, and an unshakable belief in forward movement. Even when startled by the Snake and pushed back a place, the Horse did not stop, or complain. He finished because finishing was who he was.

The Horse teaches that progress belongs to those who keep moving when things don't go as planned—that energy, courage, and consistency carry their own kind of power.

In the rhythm of time, the Horse reminds us that momentum creates destiny, and that believing in motion—and acting on it again and again—can shape an entire life.

In myths and legends, horses are often messengers between worlds, companions of heroes, and symbols of speed, freedom, and power. Some are glowing and heavenly, born from clouds or fire. Others are feared—wild, unstoppable forces that test human courage. From sacred horses that carry gods, to loyal steeds that choose their riders, cultures separated by oceans imagined horses as beings that move between the ordinary and the extraordinary.

As we look at these myths, patterns begin to appear. Horses often stand for movement and change, bravery and independence, and the pull between being guided and being free. Through these stories, people around the world used horse legends to understand strength, destiny, and the wild spirit—not just in the world, but inside themselves too.

Now, let us journey through some of the most enchanting and mythical (and some frightening) horses ever told in stories and legends.

Bayard: The Horse Who Carried Four Knights

Origin: France (Medieval romance)

Bayard was a magical horse that carried four fully grown knights at once and understood human language.

Why it enchants:

- He chooses loyalty–Bayard is more than a warhorse. He stands with the four brothers through danger and exile, showing a loyalty that cannot be forced.
- He carries four as one–His impossible strength unites four brothers.
- He moves between worlds–Part animal, part magic, Bayard feels like a bridge between the human world and the realm of legend.
- He cannot be conquered–Even when a king orders him destroyed, Bayard breaks free and disappears into the forest, a lasting symbol of freedom.

Bayard: The Horse That Carried Four Brothers

Long ago, in the deep forests of the Ardennes, where mist hung low between ancient trees, there lived a remarkable horse named Bayard.

Bayard was a large and powerful horse with a rich chestnut coat that shone in the sunlight. His mane and tail were thick and dark, and his body was broad and muscular like a warhorse. His eyes were alert and almost human in their intelligence. When he ran, his hooves struck the ground like thunder.

The horse came into the care of Renaud, the eldest of four brothers known as the Sons of Aymon. The brothers were knights—brave, proud, and raised with one simple rule above all others:
Stand together.
Where one brother went, the others followed.
And Bayard carried them all.

Beyond his loyalty and strength, Bayard had another remarkable gift. When needed, he could grow larger, stretching his powerful back so all four brothers could ride together into battle like a single moving fortress. When they galloped across the fields, it looked as if the wind had taken the shape of a horse.

The brothers were also known for their loyalty just like Bayard. For many years, the brothers served their king faithfully—until the day of the duel.

It was meant to be ceremonial—a contest of honor before nobles and banners. Renaud faced the king's nephew, a proud young prince eager to prove himself.

Duels are dangerous, even when they begin as tests of honor.
Steel rang against steel.
The crowd cheered.

Renaud fought with control and discipline, but the fight turned in a single moment. His strike landed, and the prince fell.
When the prince hit the ground and did not rise again, the entire crowd fell silent.

The king's grief turned quickly to rage.
In a single night, the brothers were declared traitors.
Their lands were seized. Their names cursed.
And the hunt began.
Across valleys and rivers, the king's army pursued them.

But the brothers had Bayard.
Through dense forests and over rocky hills, the magical horse carried them faster than any soldier could ride. Arrows whistled past them in battle, yet Bayard never stumbled.

One night, the brothers reached the edge of a great cliff.
Behind them thundered the king's cavalry, and before them stretched a river gorge so wide that even the bravest horse would refuse the leap.
The soldiers slowed.
They believed the chase was over.

But Bayard stepped forward.
His muscles tightened. His breath rose like smoke in the cold air.
Then the great horse leapt.
For a moment, the four brothers felt nothing beneath them but wind and sky.
Then Bayard landed safely on the far side.

The soldiers could only stare in disbelief as the fugitives disappeared into the forest.

From that day forward, the legend spread:
No prison could hold the Sons of Aymon while Bayard carried them.

Years passed, and many battles were fought.
But the king never forgot what had happened.
One day he offered peace to the brothers.
But the peace came with one terrible condition.
The king demanded Bayard.

Without their horse, the brothers would lose the one ally who had never abandoned them.

Yet if they refused, the war would never end.
With heavy hearts, they agreed.

Bayard was led to a river where soldiers tied a massive stone around his legs.
At the king's command, the soldiers shoved Bayard into the Meuse River.
The stone pulled him down.
The water swallowed him.
The brothers could not bear to watch and turned away.

But the story did not end there.
Far downstream, the ropes loosened.
The stone slid away.
Then, from the dark river, Bayard surged back to the surface—alive and powerful as ever.

He vanished into the forests of the Ardennes, but legend says he still runs free.
And sometimes, when the wind rushes through the valleys and echoes against the cliffs, travelers swear they hear the thunder of four riders galloping together once more.

Buraq:
The Night Journey Steed

Origin: Islamic tradition

Buraq is a radiant, winged steed who carried the Prophet Muhammad on the Night Journey (Isra and Mi'raj) from Mecca to Jerusalem and through the heavens.
Neither fully horse nor angel, Buraq moves at the speed of light.

Why it enchants:

- A bridge between Earth and Heaven, linking the human and the divine
- A symbol of spiritual ascent, not conquest or speed
- Represents guidance and trust—moving by purpose, not force
- Embodies reverence and humility in a sacred journey

Buraq: The Steed of Lightning

Long ago, in the desert lands of Arabia, there stood a city called Mecca.
Mecca was unlike any other city. For centuries, travelers had crossed deserts and mountains to reach it.

At the heart of the city stood the Kaaba, a sacred sanctuary that people came to visit in prayer and reflection.

Caravans—groups of merchants, animals, and guards—were traveling together across deserts and dangerous routes, filling the busy streets during the day. Merchants traded spices, cloth, and precious goods brought from distant lands.
But when night fell, the desert winds grew quiet, and the city rested beneath a sky filled with brilliant stars.

It was on one such night that something extraordinary happened.
The Prophet Muhammad was resting when suddenly the stillness of the night seemed to glow with light.

Before him stood the angel Jibril, a messenger sent from heaven.
"Peace be upon you," said the angel.
Behind him stood a creature unlike anything seen on earth.

It was white as moonlight and graceful as a deer. Soft wings rested along its sides. Its eyes shone with intelligence and calm.

This was Buraq.
Its name meant "lightning."
Because when Buraq moved, it traveled faster than the eye could follow.

"Tonight," said Jibril, "you will take a journey unlike any other."
Buraq lowered itself gently, inviting the Prophet to climb onto its back.
The moment he did, the creature leapt forward. In a flash, the desert disappeared behind them.

With each stride, Buraq traveled farther than a human could see. Mountains passed in an instant. Rivers shimmered beneath them like silver threads.
Above them, the stars sparkled like lanterns hung across the sky.

The Prophet and the angel traveled together across the night until the shining city of Jerusalem appeared before them.

There, Buraq gently stopped.
The Prophet stepped down, and Buraq waited calmly beside a sacred place.

Inside, something remarkable happened.

Great figures from history had gathered there—prophets who had come long before.

Among them were Abraham, Moses, and Jesus.
Though they lived in different times, on this special night, they stood together.
They prayed side by side.
It was a moment that reminded the world that the message of faith had been carried across generations.

Outside, Buraq waited patiently, its wings folded neatly, its bright eyes watching the quiet night.
The journey was not finished yet.
After the prayers, the angel Jibril spoke again.
"Now the journey continues."

Together, they began the ascent into the heavens.
Through the first heaven… and then the second… and then the third.
Each level of heaven revealed new wonders—vast skies, radiant light, and angels who welcomed the traveler.

The Prophet met many prophets who had come before him.
And each greeted him with peace.

Far below, the world seemed small and quiet.

The journey showed the greatness of creation—and the closeness between heaven and earth.

When the journey was complete, the Prophet returned once more to where Buraq waited. The faithful steed bowed its head, ready for the final ride.

In a single bound, Buraq leapt again across the night sky.
Mountains passed.
Deserts flashed by.
Cities vanished beneath them.
And before the first light of dawn touched the horizon, they were back in Mecca.

The entire journey—across the earth and through the heavens—had taken place in a single night.

Since then, the story has been remembered as the Night Journey, known as Isra and Mi'raj.

And Buraq, the steed of lightning, became a symbol of something powerful:
That with faith, guidance, and courage, even the greatest journeys can begin with a single step.

Cheonma:
The Heavenly Horse

Origin: Korea

Cheonma (Heavenly Horse) is a radiant, otherworldly steed from Korean legend, most closely associated with the Silla Dynasty. Said to descend from the heavens, Cheonma carries divine authority to earth and serves as a powerful symbol of the connection between the human world and the sky above.

Why it enchants:

- A bridge between heaven and earth, linking rulers to divine will
- Often shown with wings or flame-like patterns, moving through clouds
- Represents transcendence, speed, and spiritual power
- Reflects a culture where horses were sacred partners of authority, not mere transportation

Cheonma: The Heavenly Horse

More than a thousand ago, in Korea, there stood a magnificent city called Gyeongju, the capital of the Silla Kingdom. At that time, Korea was divided into three powerful kingdoms—Silla, Baekje, and Goguryeo—that competed for land, power, and influence.

The city's streets were filled with scholars, craftsmen, warriors, and royal courtiers dressed in silk.
Tall palace roofs curved upward like wings ready to fly. Golden crowns glittered in the sunlight. Around the city rose grassy hills that looked like gentle green mountains.

But these hills were not mountains.
They were ancient royal tombs.
Inside one of them, hidden for centuries, was a mysterious image that would one day tell the story of a magical horse.

One of these tombs was called Cheonmachong, which means "The Tomb of the Heavenly Horse."
When archaeologists opened the tomb long after the Silla kingdom had faded into history, they discovered a beautiful painting on a piece of birch bark.
The painting showed a powerful white horse galloping through the sky.

Its legs stretched like lightning. Its mane flowed like clouds. And beneath its hooves were swirling patterns that looked like wind and mist.

The ancient people called this horse Cheonma, which means "Heavenly Horse."
According to legend, it was no ordinary animal. It was a magical steed that could travel between the earth and the sky.

In the days of the Silla kings, people believed the Heavenly Horse was a messenger from the heavens.
Some said it carried the spirits of great rulers.
Others believed it appeared only to those chosen by destiny.

The horse was said to run faster than storms. When it galloped across the sky, clouds parted and the wind followed behind it.

To the people of Silla, Cheonma was a symbol of strength, courage, and heavenly blessing. That is why the image of the Heavenly Horse was placed in the tomb of a king—so that even in the next world, the ruler would have a noble steed to carry him onward.

People also believed that the Heavenly Horse could run across the sky itself—between the world of humans and the world of spirits.

Its hooves never touched the ground. Instead, it ran on wind and clouds.

Today, visitors who travel to Gyeongju, a city that still stands in the southern part of Korea, can see the famous painting of Cheonma, the Heavenly Horse.

Though the Silla Kingdom has long since passed into history, the city that once served as its capital still lives on, preserving the stories and treasures of that ancient era. And among them remains the image of the Heavenly Horse of Silla—the horse that was said to run between worlds.

Kelpie:
The Shape-Shifting Water Horse

Origin: Scotland (Celtic folklore)

The Kelpie appears as a beautiful, gentle horse standing beside a river or loch. But if a traveler climbs onto its back, the Kelpie's skin turns sticky, trapping the rider as it plunges into deep water.
Sometimes it appears as a handsome young man, luring people close before revealing its true form.

Why it enchants:

- Dark fairy-tale energy—beautiful but dangerous
- A myth that warned children away from deep waters
- Explores themes of trust, temptation, and survival

Kelpie: The Horse of the Deep Waters

Far to the north, in the misty hills of Scottish Highlands, there are deep lakes called lochs.
Some lochs are so dark and still that they look like mirrors made of midnight. Mountains rise around them, and clouds drift low across the water.

For centuries, people living in the villages nearby told stories about something that lived beneath those quiet waters.
They spoke of a mysterious creature called the Kelpie.

In Scottish folklore, the Kelpie was known as a water spirit that often appeared in the shape of a beautiful horse.
But the villagers always warned:
If you ever see a lonely horse standing beside a dark loch, do not climb onto its back.

The Kelpie often appeared on foggy evenings.
At first, it looked like an ordinary horse—a strong black horse with a smooth, shining coat, standing quietly at the edge of the water. Its mane hung wet and heavy, as if it had just stepped out of the loch.

Nothing about it seemed dangerous.

To a passerby, it might look like a lost farm horse that had wandered too close to the shore. Tired travelers might even feel tempted to approach it… perhaps to pat its neck, or climb onto its back for a ride.

But the Kelpie was never what it seemed.
Those who knew the old stories noticed something strange.
The horse never moved far from the water.
And its hooves left no sound on the ground.

According to legend, the Kelpie had a dangerous secret.
Anyone who climbed onto its back would find that they could not get off again.
Their hands would stick fast, as if glued to the creature's mane.
Then the horse would suddenly leap forward and race straight into the loch—diving beneath the dark water and disappearing into the depths.

Because of this, elders in Scottish villages told children the story of the Kelpie as a warning:
Stay away from deep waters, especially when you are alone.

The Kelpie was not always a horse.
Some stories say it could change shape.
It might appear as a handsome young stranger standing by the water.

Or as a friendly pony grazing in the mist.

But there was always one clue.
Those who looked closely sometimes noticed water weeds tangled in its hair, or the sound of dripping water even when the ground was dry.
That was how people knew the creature came from the loch.

Today, many people see the Kelpie not just as a frightening creature, but as part of the rich storytelling traditions of Scotland.

The legends reminded children to be careful around dangerous lakes and rivers.
And they filled the quiet landscapes with mystery and imagination.

Even now, when the fog rolls over a dark loch in the Scottish Highlands, some visitors still remember the old warning:
If you see a lonely horse standing by the water...
It might not be a horse at all.

It might be the Kelpie, waiting silently beneath the mist.

Longma:
The Dragon Horse of Wisdom

Origin: China

Longma (Dragon Horse) is a legendary creature from Chinese mythology, combining the body of a horse with the scales and power of a dragon. Said to emerge from rivers or the sea, Longma appears at moments of great change, bringing wisdom from heaven to the human world.

Why it enchants:

- A fusion of horse and dragon, uniting movement with cosmic power
- A messenger of heavenly wisdom and sacred knowledge
- Associated with rivers, emergence, and transformation
- Symbolizes balance between strength and intellect

Longma: The Dragon Horse of the Yellow River

Across northern China flows one of the most famous rivers in the world: the Yellow River. The Yellow River still flows today, stretching more than 3,000 miles across China before reaching the sea. For thousands of years, it has carried golden-colored silt from distant mountains, which is why its waters often appear yellow.

Long before modern cities and highways existed, the Yellow River was already the heart of ancient Chinese civilization. Early farmers built villages along its banks because its floods made the land rich and fertile for growing crops.
Many historians call it "the cradle of Chinese civilization."

But the river was more than a source of life. It was also the birthplace of many ancient legends.
And one of the most mysterious stories tells of a magical creature that once rose from its waters—the Dragon Horse, known in Chinese as Longma.

The name Longma comes from two Chinese words:
"Long" (龙) meaning dragon,
and "Ma" (马) meaning horse.

According to ancient Chinese stories, the Longma was a magical creature that combined the strength of a horse with the power and wisdom of a dragon.
Its body was shaped like a powerful horse, but its scales shimmered like a dragon's armor. Its mane flowed like clouds, and when it moved, it seemed to glide across water and sky.

The Longma was not just a strange animal. It was believed to be a messenger of heaven. One famous legend tells that the Longma, the dragon-horse, rose from the waters of the Yellow River during the time of the ancient sage Fu Xi.

Fu Xi is remembered in Chinese tradition as one of the earliest wise rulers. Stories say he taught people how to fish with nets, hunt in organized groups, and live together peacefully as families and communities. He was also known for carefully observing nature —watching the movements of the sun and moon, the patterns of rivers, and the changing seasons.

One day, as he stood beside the river, the waters stirred. From the golden current emerged a magnificent creature.
It was the Longma.

Across its back was a mysterious pattern of black and white markings—symbols that looked like a hidden map.
Fu Xi studied these patterns and used them to create the Eight Trigrams, symbols that helped people understand the hidden patterns of the natural world.
These ancient symbols later became part of the famous book of wisdom known as the I Ching.

The story was passed down from generation to generation, and the Longma became a symbol of wisdom, harmony, and guidance from the heavens.

Its image appears in paintings, carvings, and stories. Even today, it reminds people that sometimes the greatest discoveries come from watching the patterns of the world carefully—just as Fu Xi did beside the river long ago.

And in the legends of ancient China, when the waters of the Yellow River shimmer in the sunlight, some say the Dragon Horse may still be there… waiting beneath the surface, carrying the wisdom of the nature on its back.

Nuckelavee:
The Skinless Horse Demon

Origin: Orkney Islands (Scotland)

Nuckelavee is a dark, otherworldly horse spirit from Scottish (Orcadian) folklore, born of the sea and storms. Said to rise from the ocean's edge, it represents the wild, untamed forces of nature and the dangers humans cannot fully control.

Why it enchants:

- A symbol of nature's darker power, especially storms and the sea
- Represents fear of the unknown and forces beyond human command
- Blurs boundaries between land and ocean, horse and spirit
- Appears as a warning, not a guide—teaching respect for nature
- Reminds us that not all mythical horses are helpers; some are tests of courage

Nuckelvaee: The Terror of the Northern Sea

Far north of mainland Scotland, surrounded by the cold waters of the North Sea, lie the rugged islands of Orkney.
The winds there are strong, the cliffs are steep, and the sea is rarely calm. For generations, fishermen and farmers lived close to the ocean, watching the skies and tides carefully.

Life on the islands depended on the sea—but it also inspired many strange and powerful stories.
Among the most frightening legends told in Orcadian folklore was the tale of a terrifying creature known as the Nuckelavee.
People whispered its name carefully, for fear of attracting its attention.

People believed that the Nuckelavee was a monster from the sea. But unlike many sea creatures, it did not live entirely underwater. On dark nights, people claimed they saw it crawling out of the ocean and wandering across the land.

It as a horrifying sight.
The creature had the body of a powerful horse, but instead of skin, its muscles were said to be exposed, glistening like wet ropes beneath the moonlight.

On its back sat a twisted rider whose body seemed fused with the horse itself, as though the two were one terrible creature.
Worst of all, the Nuckelavee had no skin to cover its face, and its breath carried a terrible smell that could spread sickness and ruin crops.

In old Orkney stories, people believed the Nuckelavee brought trouble wherever it went. When crops failed, when animals grew sick, or when strange illnesses spread through villages, people believed it was because the creature had risen from the sea.
It was also blamed for storms that wrecked fishing boats and waves that battered the cliffs.

For island communities that depended on the land and sea, the Nuckelavee became a symbol of the dangers that could arrive without warning.

But the Nuckelavee had one critical weakness—it could not cross fresh water. Even a small stream could stop it.
One night, a man encountered the creature on a lonely road near the shore. The Nuckelavee saw him and gave chase.
Its hooves thundered across the ground as it closed the distance.
Fearing for his life, the man ran with all his strength toward a nearby stream.

Just as the monstrous creature lunged, its long, skeletal arms stretching toward him, the man threw himself across the stream. Behind him, the Nuckelavee skidded to the edge of the water. Its burning eyes glared from its twisted, skinless face as it reached forward, claws scraping the ground.

But it could go no further.
The creature reared back and roared with fury, its muscular horse body stamping the earth.
The stream—thin and quiet—had stopped the demon.
The man escaped, and the story was told again and again across the islands.

Today, the islands of Orkney are peaceful places where visitors come to see ancient ruins, seabirds, and dramatic coastlines.
But the old legends have not disappeared.
The story of the Nuckelavee reminds people of how mysterious and powerful the sea can be.

And when the wind howls across the dark northern waters, some islanders still remember the old warning:
Stay far from the shore on stormy nights.
For somewhere in the deep, the Nuckelavee may still be waiting.

Pegasus:
The Winged Horse of Inspiration

Origin: Ancient Greece

Pegasus is the legendary winged horse of Greek mythology, born from the sea and sky at a moment of great transformation. Rising from the blood of Medusa, Pegasus became a symbol of inspiration, freedom, and the power of imagination.

Why it enchants:

- A symbol of freedom and flight, rising beyond earthly limits
- Represents inspiration and creativity, especially in art and poetry
- Connects earth, sea, and sky, moving between worlds with ease
- Chosen by heroes but never owned, valuing independence
- Reminds us that imagination can lift us beyond what seems possible

Pegasus: The Winged Horse of the Sky

Today, Greek mythology continues to fascinate people around the world. These ancient stories tell of powerful gods, daring heroes, mysterious creatures, and magical adventures that shaped how the ancient Greeks understood their world. Through these myths, people imagined how storms were created, why the seasons changed, and how courage, wisdom, and pride could shape a person's fate.

According to Greek mythology, powerful gods lived high above the world.
Their home was the shining mountain called Mount Olympus.
From its snowy peaks, the gods watched over humans, storms, seas, and the changing seasons.

The world of Greek legends was also home to extraordinary creatures.
And among the most beautiful of them all was a horse that could fly.

His name was Pegasus.
He was no ordinary horse. His birth was tied to one of the most famous monsters of all—Medusa, a terrifying creature whose hair was made of living snakes. Anyone who looked directly into her eyes would instantly turn to stone.

To stop her, the hero Perseus set out on a dangerous quest. Using a polished shield as a mirror so he would not look at her directly, he crept toward Medusa while she slept. With a swift strike, Perseus defeated the monster.

But the moment Medusa fell, something astonishing happened.
From the place where she fell, a magnificent horse burst into existence.
His coat shone white as clouds.
Great wings spread from his sides.
This was Pegasus, the winged horse of legend.
With a powerful leap, he spread his wings and soared into the sky, rising high above the earth and beginning a story that would carry him among heroes and gods.

Pegasus flew freely across the skies above Ancient Greece.
His wings carried him higher than mountains and faster than the wind.
Sometimes he landed beside clear mountain springs. Other times, he galloped across the clouds themselves.

Where Pegasus struck the ground with his hooves, fresh springs of water were said to appear.
One of these springs became sacred to the Muses, who inspired poets, artists, and storytellers.

Because of this, Pegasus became a symbol of creativity and imagination.

One day, a brave hero named Bellerophon managed to tame Pegasus with the help of the goddess Athena.
Together, the hero and the winged horse flew across the skies on many adventures.

Their most famous battle was against the terrifying fire-breathing monster called the Chimera.
From high above the creature, Bellerophon was able to defeat it, thanks to Pegasus's speed and power.
The winged horse had become a partner in heroic legend.

In the end, Pegasus returned to the gods.
The great god Zeus placed the winged horse among the stars as a constellation so that people would always remember him.

Even today, on clear nights, you can still see Pegasus shining in the sky.

Sleipnir: The Eight-Legged Horse of Norse Mythology

Origin: Scandinavia (Norse mythology)

Sleipnir is the legendary eight-legged horse of Norse mythology, ridden by the god Odin. Faster than any other steed, Sleipnir can travel across land, sea, and sky—and even between the worlds of the living and the dead.

Why it enchants:

- Known for eight legs, symbolizing unmatched speed and power
- A traveler between worlds, crossing boundaries others cannot
- Represents wisdom gained through journey, not comfort
- Reminds us that true power is the ability to move forward through the unknown

Sleipnir: The Eight-Legged Horse of the Gods

Today, the northern lands of Scandinavia are known for their wild mountains, deep forests, and icy seas. In winter, the nights grow long and cold, and shimmering ribbons of light—the aurora borealis, or northern lights—sometimes dance across the sky. For ancient people living in these rugged lands, nature felt powerful, mysterious, and alive.

Long ago, inside wooden halls warmed by roaring fires, the Vikings gathered to share stories. They spoke of mighty gods who ruled the skies, fearless warriors who sailed across stormy oceans, and mysterious creatures that roamed forests, mountains, and hidden worlds.
These ancient tales are what we now call Norse mythology.

The Vikings believed the universe was far larger than the land they could see. Beyond their own world were many others—realms of gods, giants, elves, and spirits. All of these worlds, they said, were connected by a colossal cosmic tree called Yggdrasil, whose branches stretched across the heavens and whose roots reached deep into the unknown. Traveling between these worlds was no easy task.

But one creature could run across all of them.
A horse unlike any other.
His name was Sleipnir.

Sleipnir belonged to the great god Odin, the ruler of the gods.
At first glance, Sleipnir looked like a powerful gray horse.
But if you looked closely, you would notice something astonishing.
He had eight legs.
With twice the legs of an ordinary horse, Sleipnir could run faster than any creature in the world. His hooves thundered like drums across the sky, across mountains, and even across the surface of the sea.

The story of how Sleipnir was born is one of the strangest tales in Norse mythology.
Long ago, the gods hired a mysterious builder to construct mighty walls around their heavenly city of Asgard.
The builder had a powerful stallion who helped him move enormous stones.

But the gods grew worried that the builder might finish the walls too quickly and demand a great reward.
So the clever trickster god Loki created a clever plan.
Loki transformed himself into a beautiful mare and distracted the builder's stallion.

From this strange adventure came a magical foal.
That foal would grow into Sleipnir—the greatest horse in all the worlds.
When Sleipnir grew strong, he became the trusted steed of Odin.

Together, they traveled across the nine worlds of Norse mythology.
Sleipnir could gallop across the sky faster than the wind.
He could run over oceans without sinking.
He could even travel to the mysterious land of the dead known as Hel.

Because of this, the Vikings believed Sleipnir was the finest horse that had ever existed.
A horse powerful enough to carry a god.
Even after the age of the Vikings had passed, the story of Sleipnir continued to be told.
The eight-legged horse became a symbol of speed, strength, and magical journeys between worlds.

In ancient carvings, poems, and sagas, Sleipnir gallops beside Odin across the sky.
And when thunder rolls across the mountains of Scandinavia, some storytellers like to imagine it is the sound of eight mighty hooves racing across the clouds.

Trojan Horse:
The Horse That Ended a War

Origin: Ancient Greece

The Trojan Horse is a legendary wooden horse from ancient Greek history and epic storytelling, famously described in The Iliad and later Greek sources. Built as a clever deception during the Trojan War, it blurs the line between myth and history.

Why it enchants:

- A symbol of cleverness and strategy over strength
- Blurs the boundary between history and myth
- Shows how appearances can hide deeper truths

Trojan Horse: A Gift That Brought Down a City

Long ago, in the ancient world of Greece and Asia Minor, a great war was fought between two powerful cities—the Greeks and the city of Troy.
The war began after a prince of Troy named Paris sailed to Greece and took Helen, the beautiful wife of the Greek king Menelaus, back with him to Troy.
Enraged by this insult, the Greek kings gathered their armies and sailed across the sea to bring Helen home. Thousands of warriors crossed the waters in hundreds of ships, landing on the shores outside the mighty walls of Troy.

But Troy was a powerful city. Its stone walls were tall and strong, and its defenders were brave. Year after year, the Greeks tried to defeat the Trojans, yet neither side could claim victory.
For ten long years, the war continued. Battles raged outside the city gates. Great heroes fought on both sides. And still, the walls of Troy stood unbroken.

Then, at last, the Greeks came up with a plan—one of the most clever and surprising tricks in all of history.
It involved a giant wooden horse.

The Trojan Horse.

One gray morning, the people of Troy climbed the ramparts and looked toward the sea.
The Greek camps were gone.
No tents.
No ships on the shore.
No smoke from cooking fires.
The enemy had vanished.

But in the empty field outside the city stood a single object. It was a wooden horse so large that it cast a shadow across the grass. Its flanks were towering and hollow, built from massive timbers. Wheels were fixed beneath its feet, as if it had been rolled into place. Strange carvings ran along its sides—offerings to the gods.

The Trojans gathered around it in awe.
"Perhaps it is a gift," some said.
"A tribute to the goddess Athena so the Greeks may sail home safely."
Others were uneasy.
A priest named Laocoön stepped forward, his brow dark with suspicion.
"Fools!" he warned.
"Do you not see the trick? Whatever it is—I don't trust the Greeks, even when they bring gifts!"
To prove his point, he hurled his spear into the horse's side.

The spear struck the wood.
For a brief moment, the hollow body echoed—a dull, hidden sound from deep inside.
Some Trojans paused.
But the crowd quickly dismissed it.

Just then, soldiers dragged forward a captured Greek. His name was Sinon.
Trembling, he told the Trojans a carefully crafted story.
He claimed the Greeks had built the horse as a sacred offering to the goddess Athena. If the Trojans destroyed it, he warned, the goddess would curse their city. But if they brought it inside the walls, Troy would gain her protection.

The story spread quickly through the crowd.
A gift from the gods.
Against the fading protests of Laocoön, the Trojans made their decision.
The horse would enter Troy.

That evening, ropes were tied around the giant statue.
Hundreds of men pulled.
The wheels creaked.
Slowly, triumphantly, the horse rolled through the massive gates of the city.
Children ran beside it. Musicians played.

The Trojans laughed and celebrated what they believed was the end of the war.

The gates closed behind them, and night slowly fell over the city.
Unbeknownst to the Trojans, hidden deep inside the wooden horse, the greatest Greek warriors waited in silence.

Among them were heroes like Odysseus, the mastermind of the plan, and Menelaus, king of Sparta.
They had not moved for hours.
Not a breath louder than the creak of wood.
Outside, the sounds of Troy drifted upward—singing, feasting, wine flowing after a decade of war.

As the night deepened, the city grew quiet.
Then, carefully, Odysseus lifted the hidden panel.
Cold night air slipped inside.
One by one, the warriors climbed down the rope into the sleeping city.
They slipped quietly through the dark streets until they reached the gates of Troy.
The guards, tired from drinking and celebrating late into the night, were sound asleep.
The bolts slid open.

Far out at sea, hidden beyond the horizon, the Greek fleet had been waiting for this moment. Finally, the ships returned to the shore for the final attack.

Thousands of soldiers poured through the open gates.
By dawn, Troy was burning.

The mighty city that had resisted armies for ten long years fell in a single night—not by strength, but by cunning.

And ever since, the Trojan Horse has become a warning remembered through the ages:
The greatest dangers rarely arrive as open enemies. More often, they enter quietly—disguised as gifts we are eager to accept.

Tulpar:
The Steppe's Winged Horse

Origin: Central Asia (Turkic mythology)

Tulpar is a legendary winged horse from Turkic mythology, celebrated across Central Asia. Swift and powerful, Tulpar is often linked to heroic journeys, freedom, and the unbreakable bond between a rider and their steed.

Why it enchants:

- A symbol of speed and freedom, carrying heroes across vast lands
- Often shown with wings, blending earthbound strength with the sky
- Represents heroic spirit and courage in battle and travel
- Embodies the idea that true strength comes from movement, trust, and purpose

Tulpar: The Winged Horse of the Endless Steppe

Far across the heart of Central Asia, the land stretches so wide that the horizon seems to go on forever.
These endless grasslands are called the steppe—a vast open world of rolling grasses and sweeping winds, where trees are rare and the sky feels bigger than anywhere else on Earth.

The wind moves freely across the plains, and the blue sky arches like a great dome above the land.
In many places, a rider can travel for days without seeing a mountain, a forest, or a city—only waves of grass rippling beneath the sun.

For thousands of years, people journeyed across these open lands on horseback. They followed their herds as the seasons changed, living as nomads who moved from place to place, carrying their homes and stories with them across the steppe.

Among the people of the steppe—especially in the lands we now call Kazakhstan—horses were far more than animals.
They were loyal companions, swift travelers, and symbols of courage and freedom.

And in their legends, there was one horse greater than all the others.
A magical steed known as Tulpar.
Tulpar was no ordinary horse.
It looked strong and swift like the finest stallion—but from its sides grew great wings.
When Tulpar galloped, its hooves barely touched the earth.

Sometimes it raced across the endless grasslands faster than the wind. Other times it rose into the sky, soaring above mountains, rivers, and clouds.

Tulpar was said to appear only to the bravest riders.
In the legends, the winged horse could carry warriors across impossible distances in a single night—leaping rivers and climbing mountain passes where no ordinary horse could travel.

But Tulpar was more than a creature of speed.
It was said to understand the thoughts of its rider, sensing commands before a word was spoken. With only a thought or a touch, the horse would turn, climb, or race forward.
Together, horse and hero moved as one.

Across the vast plains of the steppe, riders could travel for days without reaching the horizon.

The endless wind, the open sky, and the rolling grasslands made the world feel boundless.
The winged Tulpar came to symbolize that spirit—freedom, courage, and the dream of riding wherever the wind might lead.

Even today, the legend of Tulpar lives on in Kazakhstan. Two winged horses appear on the country's national emblem, honoring the ancient stories of the steppe.

And when the wind sweeps across the endless grasslands of Central Asia, somewhere beyond the horizon, a winged horse might still be racing across the sky.

Uchchaihshravas: The King of All Horses

Origin: India (Hindu mythology)

Uchchaihshravas is a magnificent celestial horse from Hindu mythology, born during the great churning of the cosmic ocean. Pure white and radiant, he is considered the king of horses and is often associated with the god Indra, ruler of the heavens.

Why it enchants:

- Born from a cosmic event, linking him to creation itself
- A symbol of purity, nobility, and divine order
- Considered the king of all horses, not by force but by presence
- Represents heavenly authority and balance, and excellence that rises naturally, not through competition

Uchchaihshravas: The Hindu King of Horses

Long ago, in the ancient land of India, people shared stories that explained the mysteries of the universe—how the world was created, how gods shaped the heavens, and how powerful creatures came into existence. These ancient stories are part of what we now call Hindu mythology.

Many of these legends tell of a time when gods and cosmic beings worked together to uncover hidden treasures of the universe. One of the greatest of these stories began not on land, but deep within the cosmic ocean. And from those waters would emerge a horse unlike any other.
His name was Uchchaihshravas.

In one of the most famous stories of Hindu mythology, the gods and powerful beings known as Asuras were seeking treasures hidden deep within the cosmic Ocean of Milk—mysteries and wonders that had been waiting since the beginning of time.

They worked together in a great event called Samudra Manthan, the churning of the ocean. To reveal the treasures, a mighty mountain was placed at the center as the churning rod, and a giant serpent was wrapped around it like a rope.

The gods pulled from one side, the Asuras from the other, turning the mountain again and again.
The ocean roared and swirled. Waves rose high, and the waters shimmered with strange light.

And from the depths of the churning sea, marvelous treasures began to appear—radiant jewels, sacred plants, divine beings, and magical creatures the world had never seen before.

But there was more. Rising from the shining foam, came a magnificent horse.
The horse that emerged from the cosmic ocean was dazzling to behold.
His coat was pure white, shining brighter than moonlight.
Some ancient texts describe him as having seven magnificent heads, each moving with grace and power.

This was Uchchaihshravas, the most splendid horse in all the worlds.
Because of his beauty, strength, and divine origin, he was known as the king of horses.

Among the gods who witnessed his appearance was the powerful sky god Indra.
Indra chose Uchchaihshravas as his royal steed.

As the mount of Indra, Uchchaihshravas became a symbol of royal power and divine authority.
The magnificent horse carried the king of the gods across the heavens, swift as lightning and strong as thunder.

In ancient Indian art and stories, Uchchaihshravas represents strength, purity, and divine beauty.
Because he was born from the cosmic ocean itself, people believed he carried the power of creation within him.

Even today, the story of Uchchaihshravas continues to live on in the rich traditions of India. His tale appears in ancient texts such as the Mahabharata and the Puranas, and the great churning of the ocean—Samudra Manthan—is still remembered in temples, festivals, paintings, and storytelling across the country.

During major Hindu festivals like Diwali, Kumbh Mela, and temple celebrations honoring the gods, the story of the churning of the cosmic ocean is often retold through art, dance, and sacred recitations. In many temples, sculptures and murals show the gods and Asuras pulling the great serpent as treasures rise from the ocean.

Uchchaihshravas, the magnificent white horse born from those divine waters, remains a symbol of strength, nobility, and heavenly beauty.

He is remembered as one of the most extraordinary mythical horses in the world—a creature said to have risen from the very depths of the universe itself.

Quick Test:
Which Mythical Horse Are You?

Answer each question by choosing the option that feels most like you!

Keep track of the letter you pick most often.

1. When faced with a challenge, you usually...

A. Leap in boldly and trust yourself
B. Protect the people you care about first
C. Think carefully before acting
D. Feel a burst of energy and excitement
E. Stay calm and move forward no matter what

2. Your friends would say you are...

A. Imaginative and free-spirited
B. Loyal and dependable
C. Wise and thoughtful
D. Passionate and intense
E. Fast-moving and ambitious

3. If you could travel anywhere, you'd choose...

A. The sky or clouds
B. Deep forests and hidden paths
C. A place filled with ancient secrets
D. Somewhere fiery, dramatic, or powerful
E. A long road where adventure never stops

4. What matters most to you?

A. Freedom
B. Loyalty
C. Wisdom
D. Inner fire
E. Achievement

5. When things get tough, your strength comes from...

A. Hope and imagination
B. Standing by others
C. Understanding the bigger picture
D. Your emotions and drive
E. Your endurance and speed

6. If you had a special power, you'd want it to help you...

A. Soar above problems and see new ideas
B. Protect friends and stand up for what's right
C. Travel between places and understand secrets
D. Shine brightly and inspire others
E. Move faster than fear and doubt

7. When working with others, you usually...

A. Bring imagination and creativity
B. Make sure no one is left behind
C. Think carefully and guide quietly
D. Bring energy and excitement
E. Keep everyone moving forward

8. What kind of story do you love most?

A. Stories about flying and dreams
B. Stories about loyalty and bravery
C. Stories about mystery and wisdom
D. Stories about heroes and fire
E. Stories about adventure and speed

9. When someone underestimates you, you...

A. Surprise them with creativity
B. Prove them wrong by staying loyal and strong
C. Stay calm and let your actions speak
D. Rise up with confidence
E. Outrun their expectations

10. If you could leave one message behind, it would be...

A. "Believe in what you can imagine."
B. "Stand by the people who matter."
C. "Think deeply before you act."
D. "Be bold. Don't dim your fire."
E. "Keep going—no matter what."

Your Mythical Horse

Mostly A — Pegasus
You are a dreamer and a flyer. Pegasus types believe in freedom, creativity, and seeing possibilities others miss.

Mostly B — Bayard
You are fiercely loyal and brave. Like Bayard, you protect others and stand up to unfair power—even when it's hard.

Mostly C — Sleipnir
You are thoughtful and wise. Sleipnir types move between worlds, seeing things from many angles before acting.

Mostly D — Cheonma
You are powered by passion and spirit. Cheonma types shine brightest when they believe in their inner fire.

Mostly E — Tulpar
You are driven, brave, and always moving forward. Tulpar types are fast learners with big dreams, believing that effort and determination can lift them higher than they ever imagined. Like Tulpar, you grow wings through courage, perseverance, and confidence.

福

Legendary Horses

In History and In Real Life

Bucephalus

- The famed warhorse of Alexander the Great, said to fear only his own shadow. Together, they conquered much of the known world, symbolizing trust, leadership, and destiny.

Marengo

- Napoleon Bonaparte's most famous mount, ridden in several major battles. Marengo became a symbol of endurance and military glory during the Napoleonic Wars.

Incitatus

- Owned by Roman emperor Caligula, Incitatus was so favored that legend says he was almost made a consul—a top government official, like a powerful elected leader—showing how power, excess, and symbolism intertwined in ancient Rome.

Red Hare

- The legendary steed of the Chinese general Lü Bu during the Three Kingdoms era, Red Hare is celebrated in the classic novel *Romance of the Three Kingdoms*. Renowned for extraordinary speed and strength, Red Hare became a lasting symbol of unmatched power, loyalty, and towering ambition.

Copenhagen

- *Ridden by the Duke of Wellington at the Battle of Waterloo, Copenhagen symbolized steadiness and resolve during one of Europe's most decisive moments.*

Comanche

- The sole survivor of the Battle of Little Bighorn, Comanche became a living memorial to fallen soldiers and a symbol of resilience and survival.

Seabiscuit

- A small, underestimated racehorse who became a national hero during the Great Depression—proof that grit and heart can defy the odds.

Secretariat

- Widely considered the greatest racehorse of all time, famous for his record-breaking Triple Crown wins and seemingly effortless power.

Traveller

- The trusted horse of Confederate General Robert E. Lee, known for calmness under fire and deep loyalty—often remembered alongside his rider.

A Hoof-Powered City:
Horses in New York's History

Before subways, taxis, and skyscrapers, horses were the engines of New York City. From the 1600s through the early 1900s, nearly every part of daily life—transportation, trade, policing, firefighting, and even garbage collection—depended on them.

In the 1800s, New York was home to tens of thousands of horses. Streets echoed with hoofbeats, stables lined major avenues, and entire neighborhoods were shaped around caring for and moving horses.

From morning until night, hooves clopped across cobblestone streets, bells jingled, and carriage wheels rattled past storefronts. Horses were the city's power source.

Cities themselves were built to fit horses. Streets were wide and corners gently rounded so wagons could turn and hooves wouldn't slip. Hitching posts and iron rings lined buildings like today's parking spaces, and water troughs waited along busy roads for tired animals to drink.

Many horses lived in crowded stables in special "horse districts," where they slept standing up after long days of hauling heavy loads. Their lives were hard and often short, sometimes lasting only a few years.

And horses, being horses, left behind... a lot of mess. Each one produced buckets of manure and urine every day. Multiply that by tens of thousands of animals, and you can imagine the problem. People actually worried that the city might one day be buried under piles of horse waste.

Newspapers warned of a coming "manure crisis," because no one could imagine a city without horses.

Even though the horses are gone, clues from their era still hide in plain sight.
Some old stables are still standing today, turned into homes or garages. If you look closely, you might spot stone carvings of horse heads above the doors.

In parks and quiet corners of Manhattan, there are old drinking fountains made for horses, special pavement patterns designed to keep iron horseshoes from slipping, and wide roads that were once meant for carriages, not cars.

New York was shaped by hooves.

Horses and Central Park

In the mid-1800s, in the middle of a fast-growing city packed with noise, buildings, and busy streets, a daring idea emerged: what if New York set aside a massive piece of land—not for buildings, but for breathing? A giant park in the heart of the city, designed not only for people, but for horses too.

Two visionaries, Frederick Law Olmsted and Calvert Vaux, believed a city needed space to slow down. When they planned Central Park, they rejected straight, rigid lines.

Instead, they studied how horses moved. A trotting horse, they noticed, flowed best along gentle curves. So the park's carriage roads bent and rolled like ribbons through the landscape, easing the strain on horses and turning every ride into a scenic journey.

The design went even further. The park was carefully divided into three kinds of paths: wide drives for horse-drawn carriages, soft bridle paths for riders on horseback, and separate walks just for people on foot.

Today this feels ordinary, but in the 1850s it was revolutionary. It reduced chaos, prevented accidents, and gave everyone—on two feet or four hooves—their own place to move.

By the late 1800s, Central Park had become the center of New York's horse culture. Elegant carriage parades, daily commutes, and leisurely rides filled its roads. Stone basins and fountains, including those near Cherry Hill, were built specifically to water tired horses after long journeys.

When automobiles arrived in the 20th century, horses slowly vanished from city streets—but Central Park did not erase its past. The bridle paths remained. The carriage roads transformed into scenic loops for runners and cyclists. Horse-drawn carriages still appear, like living echoes of another time.

Today, Central Park feels modern and timeless all at once. But beneath its curves and paths lies the quiet imprint of hooves—a reminder that New York's green heart was shaped first by horses, long before engines claimed the streets.

Did You Know?

- Thousands of horses once filled Central Park every day.
- In the late 1800s, horses pulled carriages, carried riders, and helped New Yorkers get everywhere—long before cars existed.
- The designers studied how horses walked, trotted, slowed down, and turned—not just maps and rulers. That's why many park roads are curvy, not straight. Gentle curves were easier on horses' legs and hooves and made rides smoother and safer.
- If a road feels unusually smooth to walk or bike on, it was probably designed with horses in mind.
- Those low stone basins weren't decorations. They were placed at horse height—like 19th-century rest stops for working animals.
- Some fountains were built for horses, not people. The Cherry Hill Fountain was once a watering stop where tired carriage horses drank and rested.
- The bridle paths you see today are over 150 years old. Wealthy riders, messengers, and even police officers once used the very same routes.

Scavenger Hunt:
When You Visit Central Park

Curving Carriage Roads
Look for wide roads that gently bend instead of going straight.
Hint: Try the big looping roads that circle the park—you'll notice they curve like a flowing river, not a straight line.

Cherry Hill Fountain
Can you imagine horses stopping here to drink after a long ride?
Hint: Search near Bow Bridge, on the west side of the lake, where carriages once paused and turned around.

Low Stone Basins
See any stone bowls that seem too low for people?
Hint: Check near old carriage routes and resting spots—if it looks perfect for a horse's head, you're on the right track.

Bridle Paths
Find the dirt paths once made just for horses.
Hint: Look along the East Side or West Side of the park—these softer, brown paths still welcome horseback riders today.

Quick Quiz: *Horses in Central Park*

1. Why did Central Park have separate paths for carriages, riders, and walkers?

A. To make the park bigger
B. To keep people and horses safe
C. To make it harder to get lost

2. Why were the carriage roads curved instead of straight?

A. To confuse horses
B. To make rides last longer
C. To help horses move smoothly and comfortably

3. What was one special purpose of the fountain at Cherry Hill?

A. Decoration only
B. A place for birds to bathe
C. A drinking spot for horses

4. Why were many of Central Park's bridges built to cross over the carriage roads?
A. So people could wave at horses below
B. To separate traffic and prevent accidents
C. To make the park look like a maze

5. What does seeing horse-drawn carriages in Central Park today remind us of most?
A. That horses were once essential to city life
B. That cars have always existed in New York
C. That Central Park was built for racing

Answers: 1-B, 2-C, 3-C, 4-B, 5-A

新春大吉

Hooves to Engines
The Horsepower Continues

In the late 1700s, an engineer named James Watt studied early steam engines and carefully watched horses at work. He measured how much work a single horse could do in a short amount of time and used that number as a comparison. He called it horsepower—a simple way to say, "This machine is as strong as this many horses."

From everyday cars to super-fast machines, horsepower connects today's engines to the animals that once powered the world, reminding us that every burst of speed has its roots in a horse's strength.

	VEHICLE TYPE	***HORSEPOWER***	***"HORSE FEEL"***
	Regular car	120–180 HP	Calm pony
	Family SUV	200–300 HP	Strong workhorse
	Sports car	350–500 HP	Galloping stallion
	Supercar	600–900 HP	Legendary race horse
	Hypercar	1,000–2,000+ HP	Mythical creature

Today, you can still see horse-drawn carriages traveling through parts of Central Park and on nearby city streets. Watching a carriage roll by can feel magical. The sound of hooves, the slow pace, and the old-fashioned look remind us of a time when horses were at the center of everyday life.

But many people now ask an important question: Is this tradition still fair to the horses?

Some argue that even with rules, rest breaks, and care, living and working in a busy modern city can be hard on animals. Traffic, noise, heat, and long hours may create conditions that are very different from the peaceful park the designers imagined long ago.

So when you see a horse-drawn carriage today, it can feel like two things at once:

- A beautiful reminder of the past
- And a sign that the city—and our relationship with animals—may be ready to change

History reminds us where we come from; the present tells us when it's time to move forward.

How Horses Became Engines: *Inspiration for Automobiles*

For thousands of years, speed, strength, and freedom were measured in hooves. When humans finally learned how to build machines that could move without animals, we didn't let go of the horse—we rebuilt it in metal.
That's why even today we measure engines in "horsepower".

And some of the most famous cars in the world were even directly inspired by horses—not just in name, but in spirit and design.

Bronco

An Untamed Wild Horse

The Bronco is named after a horse that refuses to be tamed. It was built for rough land, big adventures, and places where roads disappear.

- A bronco is a wild horse that bucks and kicks.
- The logo shows the horse mid-jump, full of energy.
- Broncos are made for mud, rocks, snow, and sand.
- It's about exploring, not racing.

Equus

Royal Ceremonial Horse

Equus is the opposite of wild—it's calm, steady, and elegant. This car is inspired by a horse trained for smooth, graceful movement.

- Equus is the Latin word for horse.
- The logo is a quiet, polished horse shape.
- The ride is smooth and peaceful, not bumpy or loud.
- Power is hidden—felt, not shown.

Ferrari

The Prancing Horse of Victory

Ferrari is like a horse that loves to run—and wants everyone to hear it coming. Born on the racetrack, Ferrari cars are built for speed, excitement, and drama.

- Ferrari's logo is a prancing horse, standing on its back legs.
- The horse came from a real World War I pilot who painted it on his plane for luck.
- Ferrari cars are famous for being loud on purpose—they're meant to roar.
- Almost every Ferrari is inspired by racing, even street cars.

Ford Mustang

A Wild Horse on Wheels

The Mustang was inspired by wild horses running across open plains—and by the idea of freedom. When it came out, it became a symbol of independence.

- Mustangs were wild horses of the American West.
- The logo shows the horse running free, not trapped.
- The car was made to feel fast, fun, and affordable.
- It became a favorite of young drivers and dreamers.

Porsche

The Horse at the Heart of Precision

Porsche is all about control, balance, and going the distance—like a well-trained horse.

- The horse on the logo comes from Stuttgart's symbol. The city's name means "stud farm."
- Many Porsches have the engine in the back, helping the car grip the road—like a horse pushing off with strong back legs.
- Porsche wins races by lasting longer, not just going faster.
- Porsche cars are built for precision, not showing off.

Quick Quiz:
Which Horse-Inspired Car Are You?

1. When you move forward in life, you prefer to...

A. Run free and figure it out as you go
B. Move with passion and flair
C. Advance carefully, with perfect control
D. Push through obstacles no matter the terrain
E. Glide forward calmly, knowing you belong

2. Others admire you most for your...

A. Independence
B. Fire and confidence
C. Discipline and reliability
D. Strength and resilience
E. Grace and authority

3. If you were a horse in legend, you would be known as...
A. The untamed wanderer
B. The blazing champion
C. The loyal war horse
D. The tireless frontier steed
E. The royal mount of kings

4. Your ideal environment is...

A. Endless highways and open skies
B. A dramatic stage where everyone watches
C. Winding roads that reward focus
D. Mountains, mud, snow—any challenge
E. Quiet luxury, calm and composed

5. When challenges appear, you usually...

A. Break away and find your own path
B. Face them head-on with intensity
C. Analyze, adjust, and endure
D. Power through without complaint
E. Remain steady—pressure doesn't show

6. Power, to you, means...

A. Freedom
B. Expression
C. Control
D. Endurance
E. Presence

Mostly A's
The Wild Mustang → **Ford Mustang**
You are untamed motion. Like the Mustang, you were never meant to stand still. Freedom matters more than polish, and the road ahead excites you more than the destination.

Mostly B's
The Fire Stallion → **Ferrari**
You are passion in motion. You don't whisper—you announce. Like Ferrari's prancing horse, your power is controlled but unmistakable. You were born to be seen.

Mostly C's
The Noble War Horse → **Porsche**
You are disciplined, loyal, and precise. Others trust you under pressure. Like the horse at Porsche's heart, you value mastery over drama—and you always finish strong.

Mostly D's
The Frontier Horse → **Ford Bronco**
You are built for the long road. Rough ground doesn't slow you—it proves you belong there. Like the Bronco, your strength shows up when conditions get tough.

Mostly E's
The Royal Steed → **Hyundai Equus**
You move with quiet authority. You don't need to prove power—people feel it when you arrive. Like Equus, you represent dignity, balance, and command.

Polo:
The Sport of Kings

Imagine soccer + hockey + horseback riding —all happening at full speed. That's polo! It's one of the oldest sports in the world, but it still feels modern, exciting, and powerful today.

Polo is one of the world's oldest and most thrilling team sports—a fast-paced game played on horseback where skill, strategy, and a deep partnership between rider and horse matter just as much as strength and speed. Often called "the sport of kings," polo blends athleticism with elegance, tradition with adrenaline.

Polo began over 2,000 years ago in ancient Persia, where it was used as military training for cavalry units. The game later spread across Asia—especially India, Tibet, and China—before British officers encountered it in India in the 19th century and helped formalize modern rules.

By the late 1800s, polo had spread to England, Argentina, and the United States, becoming both a competitive sport and a symbol of prestige.

Polo is a fast team sport played on horseback. Two teams of four riders compete to score goals by hitting a small ball through the opponent's goal using a long wooden mallet.

- Game length: Usually 4–6 chukkers (periods), each about 7 minutes
- Horses: Players switch horses between chukkers so no horse gets overworked
- Scoring: A goal is scored when the ball crosses the goal line
- After every goal: Teams switch sides to keep conditions fair
- Right of way: Safety rule—players must not cross another rider's line of travel at speed
- Fouls: Dangerous riding earns penalties (free hits from set distances)

It's a game about teamwork, control, timing, and trust between rider and horse.

Countries Most Known for the Sport of Polo

- Argentina

Often called the capital of modern polo, Argentina is famous for its world-class players and horses. Many of the best polo ponies are bred and trained here, and the sport is part of everyday culture.

- United Kingdom

Polo in the UK is rich with history and tradition. The sport became popular among British officers, and today England is home to some of the world's oldest and most prestigious polo clubs.

- United States

The U.S. is known for highly competitive national leagues. Polo is played across the country, from Florida to California, blending tradition with modern athletic training.

- India & Pakistan

These countries have deep historical roots in polo. The modern game grew from ancient horseback sports played by kings and warriors, making polo an important part of their cultural history.

Notable Organizations & Events

- United States Polo Association: governs polo in the U.S.
- Argentine Open: the most prestigious polo tournament in the world
- Guards Polo Club: iconic English polo grounds
- Palm Beach Polo: winter polo capital of the U.S.
- Polo is also played in Spain, France, Australia, South Africa, Chile, and China, with both professional and amateur leagues worldwide.

Did You Know?

- They're called "**polo ponies**," but they're not ponies. Most are full-sized horses (often Thoroughbred crosses), chosen for agility and speed.
- Players may ride 4–8 horses in a single match.
- Elite players often have an entire string of horses.
- Polo is one of the fastest sports on earth. Horses can reach speeds of 35+ mph during play.
- **The ball** is tiny but tough. Traditionally made of wood; today often plastic—about the size of a baseball.
- **Jersey numbers** have meanings. #1 is the main attacker, #4 is the defensive anchor.
- **The field** is gigantic. At 300 yards long, it's the largest playing field in organized sports.
- **Right-handed** play only. For safety, all players must hold the mallet in their right hand—even if they're left-handed.
- **Royal roots** run deep. Kings, queens, emperors, and princes have played polo for centuries.

- Polo helped shape modern horseback sports. Many riding techniques used today evolved from polo training.
- Polo is a conversation between horse and rider. The best players say the horse does half the thinking.
- The **polo shirt** was born on the field. Players needed breathable shirts with collars that wouldn't flap while riding—today, polo shirts are worn everywhere, from schools to sports to weekends out.
- **Buttons** had a purpose. The small buttons on polo shirt collars were added so collars stayed put while galloping—function turned into fashion.
- **Riding boots** became style icons. Tall leather boots designed for horseback riding inspired modern fashion boots worn in cities around the world.
- For a little fashion scavenger hunt, visit the Ralph Lauren Flagship Store on **Madison Avenue** in NYC and see how many polo clues you can spot—horses, riding boots, striped shirts, and classic sport details hidden right in the design.

Fun & Quirky Horse Facts: *From Around The World*

China

Horses were so important to emperors that entire calendars, myths, and zodiac signs were built around their power and personality.

France

One of the world's most famous riding schools treats horse training like fine art—precision, balance, and grace over speed.

Iceland

Icelandic horses have a special extra gait called the tölt—so smooth you can ride while holding a full glass of water without spilling it. Also, once an Icelandic horse leaves the country, it can never return (to protect the breed!).

Japan

Some shrines hold traditional horse festivals where horses wear colorful decorations and are honored as messengers between humans and the gods.

🇲🇳 Mongolia

There are more horses than people in Mongolia. Kids often learn to ride before they can read, and horses are still essential for daily life across the open steppe.

🇪🇸 Spain

The famous Andalusian horse is known for dancing-like movements. These horses helped inspire classical ballet poses and royal riding styles.

🇬🇧 United Kingdom

The horses guarding Buckingham Palace are trained to stay calm—even when tourists shout, cameras flash, or buses rumble past. They're basically the most polite bodyguards in the world.

🇺🇸 United States

Wild mustangs still roam parts of the West, descendants of horses brought centuries ago. They're protected as living symbols of freedom.

No matter the country, horses aren't just animals—they're athletes, partners, symbols, and sometimes even legends.

Want More?:
Horse Museums & Exhibits

United States

Kentucky Horse Park - International Museum of the Horse
Lexington, Kentucky—right in the heart of America's horse country, surrounded by rolling bluegrass farms and real working stables.

Metropolitan Museum of Art (Arms & Armor Galleries)
Upper East Side, Manhattan, New York City—along Fifth Avenue by Central Park, home to legendary armored horses and knights.

National Museum of Racing and Hall of Fame
Saratoga Springs, Upstate New York—steps away from the historic Saratoga Race Course, one of the most famous racing towns in the world.

France

Musée du Cheval
Chantilly, just north of Paris—inside a grand château surrounded by forests and royal stables once used by French nobility.

United Kingdom

Royal Armouries
Leeds, northern England—a striking modern museum beside the Leeds Dock, famous for its medieval horse armor displays.

The Message:
For the "Horse Year" Children

For as long as humans have told stories, horses have been part of them. They carried our ancestors across wide lands, helped families work and trade, and inspired legends that are still told today.

Horses taught people how to move together—how to trust, how to be brave, and how to keep going even when the road was long. Even now, their spirit is everywhere. When we talk about speed and strength, we still say horsepower.

If you were born in a Year of the Horse, this story belongs to you too. Horse-year kids are often said to be full of energy, curiosity, and courage. They like to explore, to learn by doing, and to follow their own path. Like the horse, they remind us that moving forward takes heart—not just speed.

You're in good company, too. Throughout history, the Year of the Horse has also marked the births of many powerful world figures—some admired, some feared, and some still debated today.

Throughout history, people born in the Year of the Horse have often stood out for their energy, determination, and drive. Leaders such as Genghis Khan and Theodore Roosevelt—although opinions may vary about their leadership and impact—left lasting marks on the world through bold action and momentum.

Many admired athletes, creators, and innovators were also born in a Year of the Horse, including Kobe Bryant, whose relentless work ethic inspired excellence, Jackie Chan, whose fearless creativity brought joy and adventure to audiences worldwide, and James Cameron, whose determination pushed filmmaking and exploration to new frontiers.

Across leadership, sports, and the arts, these individuals are remembered for courage, creativity, and forward motion—qualities long associated with the Horse.

So wherever life takes you—into new ideas, new places, or big dreams—remember this: You come from a long line of movement, courage, and possibility.

The world has always moved forward with horses—and now, with *you*.

Quick Quiz:
What Horse Trait Do You Have?

Pick the answer that sounds most like you. Don't overthink it!

1. When you start something new, you usually...

A) Jump in right away—learning as you go
B) Practice quietly until you feel ready
C) Think big and imagine where it could lead
D) Stick with it, even when it gets tough

2. Your friends would describe you as...

A) Energetic and always moving
B) Loyal and dependable
C) Curious and creative
D) Determined and focused

3. Your favorite kind of challenge is...

A) A fast-paced competition
B) Helping a team succeed together
C) Trying something no one's done before
D) Pushing yourself to improve

4. If something doesn't go your way, you...

A) Shake it off and try again quickly
B) Stay calm and keep going
C) Find a new, clever approach
D) Work harder until it clicks

5. Your ideal day includes...

A) Action, movement, and excitement
B) Time with people you trust
C) Creating or discovering something new
D) Reaching a goal you worked toward

Results:
Mostly A's — The Swift Horse
You're full of energy and love momentum. You learn by doing and aren't afraid to move fast.
Mostly B's — The Steady Horse
You value loyalty and reliability. People trust you because you stay calm and dependable.
Mostly C's — The Curious Horse
You're imaginative and brave about exploring new ideas. Creativity is your superpower.
Mostly D's — The Determined Horse
You don't give up easily. Your strength comes from focus, discipline, and persistence.

The Swift Horse (energy & action)
You like movement, excitement, and learning by doing.

- Athlete or coach
- Emergency responder (firefighter, EMT)
- Pilot or astronaut
- Stunt performer or action filmmaker
- Entrepreneur / startup founder
- Event planner

The Steady Horse (loyalty & teamwork)
You're dependable, calm under pressure, and great in groups.

- Teacher or school counselor
- Veterinarian or animal care specialist
- Nurse or healthcare worker
- Project manager
- Civil engineer
- Community organizer

The Curious Horse (creativity & exploration)
You love ideas, imagination, and discovering how things work.

- Artist or illustrator
- Writer or storyteller
- Architect or designer
- Scientist or inventor
- Game designer
- Film director or animator

The Determined Horse (focus & perseverance)
You thrive on goals, discipline, and long-term effort.

- Professional athlete
- Engineer or programmer
- Surgeon or researcher
- Lawyer or judge
- Classical musician
- Business leader or executive

Remember your interests will grow and change—and many people carry more than one Horse trait. The best path is the one that keeps you curious, motivated, and true to yourself.

Scavenger Hunt:
Symbols of Luck & Fortune

Throughout the book, traditional Chinese symbols of luck, fortune, and prosperity are hidden.
How many did you find? Do you know what they mean?

Red Envelope (红包 – Hóngbāo)
Meaning: Luck, prosperity, blessings
Money gifts given during Chinese New Year
Symbolizes sharing good fortune with family and children

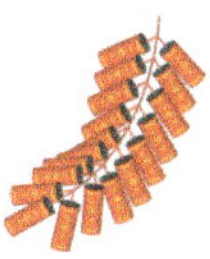

Firecrackers (爆竹 – Bàozhú)
Meaning: Protection and celebration
Loud firecrackers are set off during Lunar New Year
Believed to scare away evil spirits and bad luck

Lion Dance (舞狮 – Wǔshī)
Meaning: Courage and good fortune
Traditional dance performed during festivals
The lion brings luck and prosperity to homes and businesses

Dragon Dance (舞龙 – Wǔlóng)
Meaning: Power, strength, prosperity
A long dragon puppet carried by dancers
Symbolizes good luck and a successful year

Lantern (灯笼 – Dēnglóng)
Meaning: Hope and bright future
Red lanterns decorate homes and streets during celebrations
Represent light, joy, and good fortune

Chinese Gold Ingot (元宝 – Yuánbǎo)
Meaning: Wealth and prosperity
Ancient boat-shaped gold currency used in imperial China
Symbol of financial success and abundance

Lucky Coins (铜钱 – Tóngqián)
Meaning: Wealth and financial luck
Round coins with square holes tied with red string
Represent harmony between heaven and earth

Mandarin Oranges (橙子 – Chéngzi)
Meaning: Wealth and success
Golden oranges exchanged during New Year visits
Their color and name symbolize prosperity

Kumquat Tree (金桔 – Jīnjú)
Meaning: Good fortune and wealth
Small golden fruits displayed in homes during the holiday
The name sounds similar to "gold" in Chinese

Lucky Knot (中国结 – Zhōngguó Jié)
Meaning: Endless good luck and unity
Decorative red knot with no beginning or end
Represents lasting happiness and harmony

Paper Cuttings (剪纸 – Jiǎnzhǐ)
Meaning: Happiness and celebration
Traditional red paper designs placed on windows
Often feature animals, flowers, and lucky symbols

Spring Couplets (春联 – Chūnlián)
Meaning: Blessings for the new year
Red calligraphy banners placed beside doors
Express wishes for happiness, wealth, and success

Fish (鱼 – Yú)
Meaning: Abundance and surplus
Often served or displayed during New Year celebrations
The word for fish sounds like the word for "surplus"

Fu Character (福 – Fú)
Meaning: Good fortune and blessings
The Chinese character for luck often placed on doors
Sometimes hung upside down to mean "fortune has arrived"

God of Wealth (财神 – Cáishén)
Meaning: Wealth and prosperity
Mythical figure who brings fortune in the new year
Often shown holding gold ingots and treasure

Peach of Longevity (寿桃 – Shòutáo)
Meaning: Long life and health
Peaches associated with immortality in Chinese mythology
Common symbol in celebrations and art

Coming Up Next:
The Gracious Goat

The story doesn't end here.
Just as the Year of the Horse celebrates energy, courage, and motion, the next year brings a new kind of strength—one that shines quietly, thinks carefully, and moves with purpose.

In 2027, we enter the Year of the Fire Goat. Where the Horse charges forward, the Goat climbs patiently. Its strength is thoughtful, gentle, and steady.

Whether you're charging ahead like a Horse or climbing thoughtfully like a Goat, every path matters—and every kind of strength has its moment.

The journey continues.

ABOUT THE PUBLISHER

Bridging the Past. Inspiring the Future.

Mentor NYC is an independent content studio and publishing house based in New York City devoted to storytelling that connects generations, cultures, and ideas.

We honor timeless works while embracing the future of art, culture, and technology—telling stories that spark curiosity, deepen understanding, and invite reflection.

In a fast-paced world, we champion deep reading and meaningful engagement. Our books are built to last—intellectually, physically, and spiritually—so that as the world moves forward, its most important stories endure.

Learn more at www.mentornyc.org

Keep the adventure going!

Follow us on Instagram

@MentorNYCBooks

www.ingramcontent.com/pod-product-compliance
Ingram Content Group UK Ltd.
Pitfield, Milton Keynes, MK11 3LW, UK
UKHW060116010826
14089UKWH00003B/11

9 798998 533778